Noises of the Night

A Canadian Lullaby

By Alana Pidwerbeski

The doors have been locked
We've turned off my light
Read books with the voices
And tucked me in tight

Outside the wind blows
Through the leaves in the trees
My eyes are drooping
My mind drifting with ease

The noises of the night
Differ near, differ far
They sing you lullabies
Wherever you are.

2

By the ocean the waves
Lap against the seashore
  Or they roar and they crash
  With the rain in a storm.

Up north the wind sings
Through the whispering pines
And the night sky dances
In bright shimmering lines.

4

The snow floats down gently
Or for months it's still light

And the sun smiles down
As the clock chimes midnight.

Somewhere in the distance
A wolf howls to the moon

And elsewhere is heard
The haunting call of a loon.

6

The noises of the night
Differ near, differ far
They sing you lullabies
Wherever you are.

Out East the Cicadas
Hum in the trees
Like vibrant electricity
Buzzing like bees.

The pigeons are purring
"Coo-coo, Coo-coo"

A father is snoring
And Sister is too.

9

In cities cars rumble
As people drive by   And planes can be heard
                            As they fly through the sky.

Brick houses snuggle close
As they turn out their lights

And raccoons start to wander
As they wake for the night.

11

The noises of the night
Differ near, differ far
They sing you lullabies
Wherever you are.

On the plains hoots an owl
As it glides overhead
And the crickets are chirping
"It's time now for bed"

In the marsh a frog croaks
Its sweet lullabies
In fields cattle low
Before closing their eyes.

14

A foal huddles close
To its mother so dear
And surrenders to sleep
It has nothing to fear.

The noises of the night
Differ near, differ far
    They sing you lullabies
    Wherever you are.

In the west a bear snores
With her cub cuddled up

And a seal mum stays warm

As she snuggles her pup.

And Coyote trills out
Calling her friends

And a **"Honk"** echoes down
From geese overhead

The noises of the night
Differ near, differ far
They sing you lullabies
Wherever you are.

19

And as the night quiets
And the world shuts its eyes
Canada grows silent
While little girls and little boys

Drift off to dreamland
As Turtle Island *sleeps*
(Save for the bear snoring)
No one utters a peep.

ABOUT THE AUTHOR:

Passionate about helping children learn and grow, Alana has taught Karate to preschoolers, Nannied, and volunteered to run kids' programs at the community centre. Her Bachelor's degree combined her love of culture (Anthropology) with her love of books (Literature), but she was missing her creative side. One noisy, sleepless Toronto night, she was inspired to write *Noises of the Night* and realized that writing and illustrating books was where her heart was happiest.

Alana lives in B.C.'s sunny Okanagan Valley. When she isn't writing or painting, she can be found dancing around her house singing at the top of her lungs (much to the disappointment of her neighbours) or cooking delicious meals. She believes in hugs, holding doors open for others, and petting as many dogs as is possible.

She respectfully acknowledges that she lives and works on the traditional unceded and ancestral territory of the Syilx peoples.

◆ FriesenPress

Suite 300 - 990 Fort St
Victoria, BC, V8V 3K2
Canada

www.friesenpress.com

ISBN
978-1-5255-9016-0 (Hardcover)
978-1-5255-9015-3 (Paperback)
978-1-5255-9017-7 (eBook)

Juvenile Nonfiction, Bedtime & Dreams

Distributed to the trade by The Ingram Book Company

Printed in the USA
CPSIA information can be obtained
at www.ICGtesting.com
JSHW070101140923
48178JS00003B/20

9 781525 590160